Basic Instructions

Preparing Wood

Lightly sand and wipe wood clean before applying paint or glue.

Grungeboard

Cut Grungeboard with a craft knife or scissors (a paper cutter causes it to bend). To capture an embossed pattern, apply inks directly to the surface. Grungeboard stands up to sanding and won't break down or lose flexibility when wet.

Masks

Apply a mask to Grungeboard. Spritz with Color Wash. Removing the mask while still wet will give a softer edge. If the mask is left on until dry, the design edge will be crisp.

Gluing on Fabric

Place a sheet of heavy cardboard into garment before gluing or painting. Let dry 24-48 hours and always turn garments inside out before laundering.

Bird Plaques

by Michael Jack Putman
& Lesley Fisher

Delight the birdwatcher in your family with a truly unique gift that celebrates our feathered friends.

SIZE: 4" x 5"

MATERIALS:

idea-ology Trinkets: Grungeboard shapes, Grungeboard Elements, Corners, Clear acrylic Fragments, Salvage Stickers, Assorted Foliage, Fasteners

Ranger: Glossy Accents, Perfect Pearls, Rubber Stamp ink, Alcohol Blending Solution Alcohol Ink Applicator, Alcohol inks: Black, Butterscotch, Rust

Heidi Swapp Bird Ghost shapes

2 Wood 4" x 5" boards

Ten Seconds Studio (#5 Paper stump, Metal Tools)

Metal Tape (from the hardware store)

Sanding block

The Ultimate! glue

INSTRUCTIONS:

1. Create a design on a wood board with selected Grungeboard shapes and Bird Ghost shapes. Glue shapes in place. Let dry.
2. Cover board and shapes with strips of metal tape, alternating directions as you work.
3. Use a paper stump to burnish tape and create outlines.
4. Create texture using various metal tools.
5. Add color and antiquing by applying alcohol ink with an Applicator. Wipe off excess color from the highlights with a cloth while still wet. Let dry.
6. Lightly sand away areas of color build up.
7. Use Glossy Accents as glue. Adhere fragments as desired. Adhere circle fragment to clock sticker and rectangle to stamped word 'Bird'. Let dry.
8. Cut metal tape away from the word with a craft knife.
9. Layer foliage with brads.
10. Glue fragments, foliage and corners in place.
11. Use alcohol ink to color leaf shapes to be used for wings. Add shine by brushing on Perfect Pearls. Glue wings to birds.

1. Paint crackle on canvas with a foam brush.

2. Apply Salvage sticker sheets on the back of canvas panel.

3. Lightly sand embossed metal to reveal silver lines.

4. Glue wood trim in place.

5. Fold and assemble roof.

6. Attach canvas sides to base.

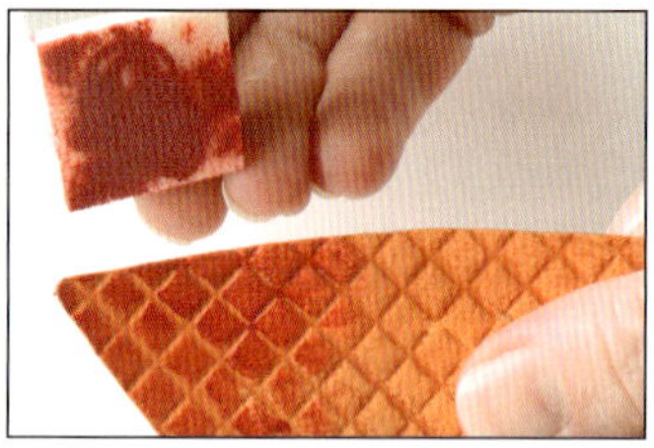

7. Paint Grungeboard heart using Cut'nDry foam.

8. Fold back the flaps of heart, staple in place.

Love is the Heart of the Home

It is so much fun and a pleasant surprise to remove the roof and reveal the explosion base with a heart in the center.

SIZE: 5" x 5½" x 10"

MATERIALS:
idea-ology Trinkets:
3 sheets Grungepaper, Grungeboard (Nature), Keyhole, Keys, Snaps, Foliage, D-Rings, Swivel clasps, Jump Rings, Corners, Word Tokens, Salvage Stickers, Tiny Attacher mini stapler
Ranger: Distress Crackle (Pine Green, Antique Linen); Adirondack Paint Dabbers (Terra Cotta, Espresso, Mushroom, White, Citrus, Red Pepper, Coral, Cranberry); Memory frames (1½" x 1½", two 1" x 3")
Ten Seconds Studio: Metals (Dijon, Mocha); Molds (BDD1a, K3b); Humungo Tape sheets)
Wood (1½" cube, 4" x 4" plaque, 24" dollhouse trim, bamboo skewer)
4 canvas 5" x 7" panels
Paper Whimsey Collage images
Scoring tool, Hole punch, Sanding block
Scallop border punch, Craft knife
Drill & small drill bit

INSTRUCTIONS:

4 Canvas Panel Walls for House:

1. Paint both sides of all canvases with a Mushroom Dabber. Let dry. Paint the top two thirds of the front of each canvas with Antique Linen Crackle paint. Let dry.
2. Cover the back of the panels with Salvage stickers.
3. Cut 4 pieces of Mocha metal $2\frac{1}{4}$" x 5". Emboss using molds. Lightly sand over the embossed area to reveal the aluminum beneath.
4. Make miniature collages to fit inside 4 memory frames. Align images in the square frames with the jump rings on the bottom so charms can be suspended.
5. Cut a Grungepaper door $2\frac{1}{2}$" x $5\frac{1}{2}$". Paint with Terra Cotta. Cut out a hole to fit the memory capsule. Tape the metal pieces to the bottom of each panel. Attach the memory frames and door.
6. Cut three 5" pieces of dollhouse trim and 2 smaller pieces to fit on each side of the door. Paint with Terra Cotta. Let dry. Attach to top of metal.

House Roof:

1. Using the pattern, cut 2 Grungepaper pieces. Adhere tape to flaps as shown. Punch holes for a handle. Score all the lines on the roof to ease the folding.
2. Paint Espresso inside the roof. Paint outside with Mushroom.
3. Cut 11 Mocha metal strips 2" x $5\frac{1}{2}$". Use a scallop border punch to shape the edges. Emboss and sand 6 strips. Tape strips to roof.
4. Add D-ring through the holes, attach charms.

House Base:

1. From Grungepaper cut a 6" x 6" base & grass.
2. To create flaps, score lines $\frac{1}{2}$" in on all sides. Cut out resulting squares on corners.
3. Paint front of flaps with Pine Crackle. Let dry. Dry brush with Citrus. Paint the center of base with Espresso. Let dry.
4. Apply tape to the base flaps and leaves. Remove protective backing from the tape, attach grass on each side. Attach each wall panel to the base, wrapping it up and around to cover the bottom stem of the grass at the house's base.
5. Add Grungeboard pieces and embellishments as desired.

House Roof Pattern
Score on dashed lines.
Enlarge pattern to 200%

Adhesive Tape

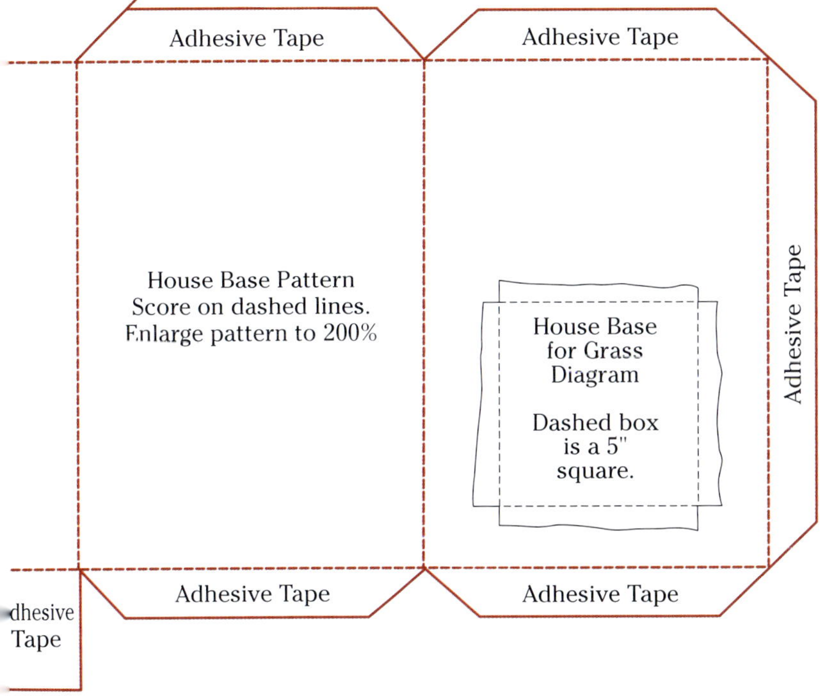

Home is Where the Heart Is

by Lisa Patterson

This delightful centerpiece opens to reveal the heart of the home. Construct a house shape with inexpensive canvas panels. Add metal, Grungeboard, photos, and trinkets for a wonderful look.

Heart Pedestal:

1. Using Espresso dabber, paint all wooden surfaces. Let dry.
2. Cut 2 Grungepaper hearts. Slice an "x" in only one piece. Paint and distress both sides of each heart.
3. Pull X apart and staple small flaps back to create the opening for a piece of metal or small charm.
4. Apply Humungo tape to the back of each heart. With a bamboo skewer sandwiched between the hearts, adhere them together.
5. Drill a small hole in the wooden block and insert the bamboo skewer to display the heart.
6. Mount the block onto the wooden plaque and attach to the center of the house base.

Creative Time Clock

by Karen Wells

Express your artistic talents with a timeless project that you will enjoy for years.

SIZE: 9" x 12"

MATERIALS:

idea-ology Trinkets:
- 4 stars & 1 oval frame from Grungeboard Elements;
- Salvage stickers ('1','2','3','9', 's', 'i','x'); Timeworks mask;
- Journaling ticket; 4 Mini Pins, 4 Sprocket Gears, Trinket Pin,
- Foliage flowers (two 5⁄8", two 7⁄8"), 2 Brass mini brads

Ranger:
- Vintage Photo Distress ink pad, Stickles (Gold, Silver)
- Distress Crackle paint (Broken China, Tea Dye)
- Adirondack (Silver acrylic paint Dabber; Color Wash: Eggplant, Plum)

Clock mechanism, 9" x 12" wood oval, Corrugated cardboard

Ten Seconds Studio (Metal: Dark Chocolate, Dijon; #5 Paper stump; Acrylic plate; Sanding block; Molds: BDAD03a, BDAD4b)

Drill, Drill bit, Soft cloth

E6000 glue, Red liner tape

INSTRUCTIONS:

1. Paint wood with crackle paints. Let dry.
2. Arrange mask on surface and mist with Color Wash. Let dry.
3. Paint Grungeboard with Silver acrylic.
4. Emboss metal with paper stump; sand; wipe clean.
5. Glue metal elements to salvage sticker numbers.
6. Outline numbers with Stickles.
7. Distress cardboard with Vintage Photo ink.
8. Tape numbers "12" and "3" to metal pieces and tape to clock face. Tape "9" to corrugated cardboard and journaling ticket; tape to clock face.
9. Glue letters "six" to clock face. Attach foliage flowers to frame with brads and glue frame to clock face. Glue stars to clock face.
10. Drill hole for clock mechanism and insert mechanism.

'Sincere' Plaque

by Darlia Hobbs

Heartfelt messages are beautifully expressed when you turn them into original art.

SIZE: 6" x 24"

MATERIALS:

idea-ology Trinkets:
- Letters from Grungeboard Alphas,
- Adage ticket, 3 Sprocket Gears,
- 'E' Stencil Type, Large Game Spinner,
- Word Token, Word Key

6" x 24" Wood plaque

1 Silver push pin

2" skeletal leaf

Krylon (18kt. Gold Leafing Pen, UV Protective Acrylic Coating)

Golden (Matte Medium, Gesso, Fluid acrylic: Purple, Turquoise, Quinacridone Nickel Azo Gold, Cream, Tan)

Black Archival ink pad

Toothpick, Paintbrushes (#4 round, 1" flat)

Combs (Wide tooth, Medium tooth)

3⁄4" circular cap of a spray bottle

INSTRUCTIONS:

1. Spray the paper word with UV Protective acrylic coating. Let dry.
2. Completely paint the wood plaque with a thin coat of White gesso. Let dry. Paint a second thicker coat. Let dry.
3. Paint a thick area of White gesso on each end of the plaque. Comb through wet gesso in a swirling motion to create a texture. Immediately press the plastic cap, open end down, into gesso; turn in a circular motion and lift. Make several circles. Let dry.
4. With tip of round brush, apply watered-down Azo Gold onto partial edge of 3 circles.
5. Paint Purple over top and sides letting White show through. Let Dry.
6. Brush Turquoise paint over Purple paint leaving some colors showing. Let dry.
7. Paint Grungeboard letters with acrylic paints. Let dry and ink the edges.
8. Drizzle Cream fluid acrylic across plaque as desired. Quickly rake a wide tooth comb through paints. While still very wet, press a few metal embellishments, word written on paper, adage ticket, and painted letters into the wet paint. Use the tip of a toothpick to press the pieces down into wet paint. Acrylic paint acts as a glue. Let dry.
9. Brush matte medium over the entire top surface. Let dry.
10. Draw dots with a Gold pen after the stencil plate "E."
11. Paint skeletal leaf lightly with Turquoise and adhere it to the plaque with matte medium. Let dry.
12. Use a small nail to make a hole for the push pin. Attach word token with push pin.

TIPS:

1. Wear protective gloves. Read all warnings on all bottles and products.
2. When working with any kind of acrylic paint, gesso, gels, or mediums, always have a water tub ready to clean your brushes and tools.
3. When leaving paints, gessos or mediums and gels open while you use them, they tend to dry and get thicker. It helps to add a few drops of clean water before you replace the lids tightly. If possible, pour a small amount of paint, etc., into a 1 oz plastic cup and use from that, instead of right out of the container. Replace lids quickly.
4. If desired, sand the ends of the plaque smooth,
5. If your paint covers too solidly, wipe the desired area with a damp cloth.

1. Paint the wood plaque with 2 coats of White gesso.

2. Paint thick gesso on each end. Comb through wet gesso.

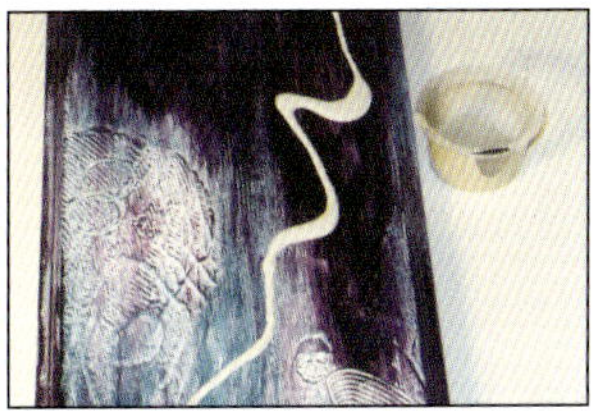

3. Paint Purple and Turquoise. Drizzle Cream across plaque.

4. Press embellishments into the wet paint. Let dry.

5. Draw dots with a Gold pen after the stencil plate "E."

6. Paint leaf lightly with Turquoise. Adhere to plaque.

Desk Storage Cabinet

by Donna Goss

Got stuff? Clean up your art room or desk with this fabulously expressive and fun cabinet. All your friends will want one.

SIZE: 8" x 11" x 14"

MATERIALS:

idea-ology Trinkets:
- Grungeboard Elements shapes; Masks (Flourish, Timeworks);
- 17 assorted acrylic Fragments, 8 Hitch Fasteners

Ranger:
- Adirondack Acrylic paint Dabbers (Lettuce, Snowcap, Gold, Silver)
- Alcohol inks (Purple, Twilight, Stream, Sunset Orange)
- Alcohol ink applicator tool, Blending tools, Cut n' Dry sponges
- Distress ink pads (Vintage Photo, Dusty Concord, Broken China, Fired Brick, Spiced Marmalade)
- Antique Linen Distress Crackle paint
- Stickles (Antique Linen Distress, Christmas Red, Silver)
- Glossy Accents glue

howdoyouglue.com Wooden cabinet 8" x 11" x 14", 8 acrylic 8" x 10" box frames
5 music sheets $5\frac{1}{2}$" x $8\frac{1}{4}$", $8\frac{1}{2}$" x 11" Cream cardstock
Liquid Nails glue, Brush for glue, The Ultimate! glue

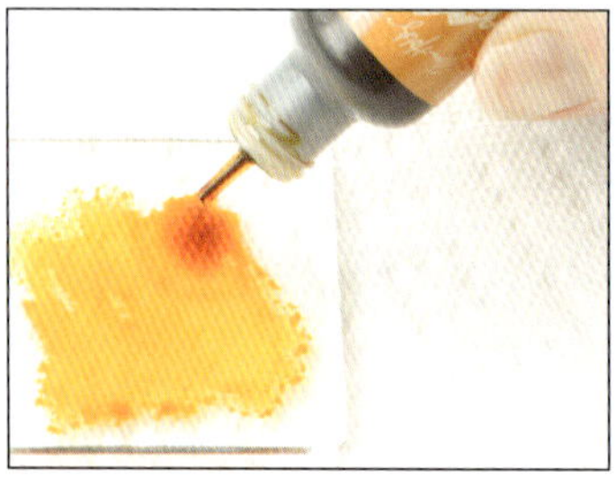

1. Drip alcohol inks onto clear acrylic fragments. Let dry.

2. Stencil small stars on the side of the cabinet with a sponge.

INSTRUCTIONS:

1. Paint cabinet inside & out using Lettuce dabber. Let dry.
2. Tear sheet music in half. Ink edges with Vintage Photo ink. Glue music to sides, back and top of cabinet.
3. **Top of Cabinet:** Lay Timeworks masks on in various places. Sponge with Broken China and Spiced Marmalade inks. Let dry.
4. **Back of Cabinet:** Lay Timeworks masks on in various places. Sponge with Broken China, Dusty Concord and Spiced Marmalade inks. Paint Grungeboard with dabbers. Let dry. Glue to cabinet with The Ultimate! Apply Stickles to painted Grungeboard. Let dry.
5. Apply alcohol inks to various acrylic fragment pieces. Let dry. Adhere to cabinet with Glossy Accents.
6. **Left Side of Cabinet:** Sponge over Flourish mask with Spiced Marmalade ink. Color Grungeboard with distress ink and edge with Vintage Photo.
7. Paint wings with Crackle. Let dry. Glue heart to wings and to cabinet with The Ultimate! Glue.
8. Apply alcohol inks to 6 fragment pieces various sizes. Let dry. Adhere to cabinet with Glossy Accents.
9. **Right Side of Cabinet:** Sponge Dusty Concord ink on the negative star grungeboard like a mask.
10. Color Grungeboard arrow with Spiced Marmalade. Edge with Vintage Photo. Paint Grungeboard label holder with Silver dabber. On Cream cardstock, print the words 'this way up'. Cut to fit and attach behind label. Glue label and arrow on to cabinet using The Ultimate! Apply Silver Stickles in holes on label.
11. Apply alcohol inks to 5 acrylic fragments. Let dry. Adhere to cabinet using Glossy Accents.
12. **Drawers:** Ink sides of each drawer with Stream alcohol ink. Attach one hitch fastener to each drawer as drawer pull using Liquid Nails. When dry slide drawers into cabinet.

Creativity Doll

by Donna Goss

For thousands of years artists have enjoyed the freedom of expression and the opportunity to show off inventive craftsmanship that comes from creating unusual dolls. This one is a great combination of collage - just for fun!

SIZE: 6" x 13½"

MATERIALS:

idea-ology Trinkets:
- 1 sheet of Grungepaper,
- Masks (Flourish, Borderline),
- 4 long brads, 2 Hitch Fasteners, Ornate plate,
- 4 Sprocket Gears, 2 Jump Rings, 2 Swivel Clasps

Ranger:
- Color Wash (Butterscotch, Stream, Lettuce)
- Distress ink pads (Mustard Seed, Fired Brick, Aged Mahogany, Broken China)
- Cut n' Dry foam, Blending tools, Mini Mister
- Glossy Accents, ¼" Red liner tape

Antique doll head, 2 brass hand charms
12" of Black 2" wide crepe ribbon
8½" x 11" of Cream cardstock,
Computer & printer, The Ultimate! glue
Sewing machine, Black thread, Awl

INSTRUCTIONS:

1. From 1 corner, measure 5" in both directions along the edge of the Grungepaper and make a mark. Connect the marks and trim away the triangle. This cut edge will be the neck portion of the cone.
2. Mist Grungepaper with water and spray Color Wash randomly. Let dry.
3. Apply masks. Using a blending tool, apply Distress ink over masks. Let dry.
4. Form a cone shape and secure with tape. Trim bottom even.
5. Glue head on small end of cone.
6. Sew a Gathering stitch across the center of the crepe paper. Gather to form a ruffle. Tape ruffle in place.
7. Computer print the word "Creativity" on Cream cardstock. Cut to fit back of ornate plate. Attach using Glossy Accents. Secure plate to body using brads.
8. Poke holes in sides of body near head for attaching hitch fasteners.
9. Remove swivel clasp and small jump ring from chain. Attach large jump ring in its place. At other end of chain, attach hand charm to small jump ring. Repeat for hand charm. Slide jump rings on hitch fasteners. Glue hands to front of body.
10. Attach layered gears with brads.

1. Mist Grungepaper with water.

2. Spray with Color Wash.

3. Shape into a cone

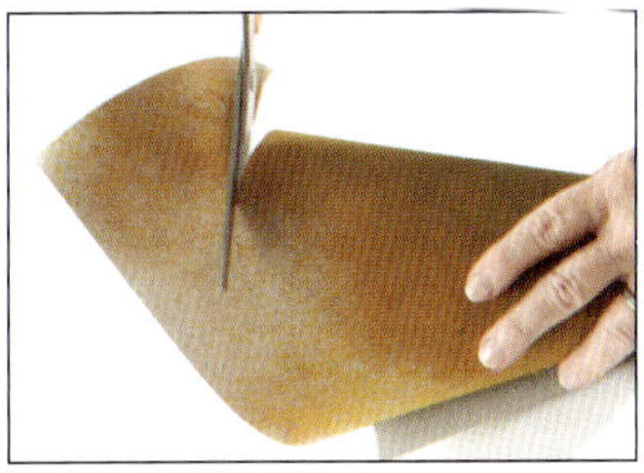

4. Cut the corner off the bottom of cone.

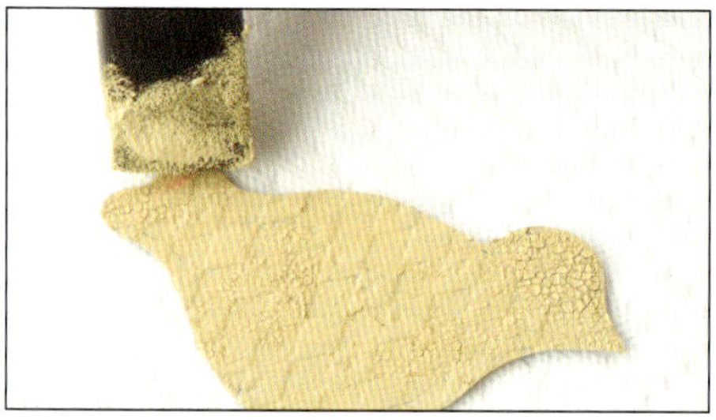

1. Paint a Grungeboard bird with Picket Fence Crackle paint. Let dry.

2. Ink the bird and music paper with Vintage Photo and Black Soot Distress inks.

3. Embellish with feathers, eggs and old jewelry pieces.

Sweet Bird Nest

by Judy Ross

It's exciting to peek into a nest to find a clutch of eggs. One marvels at the delicate fragility of this masterpiece of nature. Express your love for our feathered friends in a wonderful piece that will beautify your home.

SIZE: 3½" x 8"

MATERIALS:

idea-ology Trinkets:
Grungeboard

Ranger:
Distress inks (Vintage Photo, Black Soot)
Distress Picket Fence Crackle paint

3" x 3" frame on metal stand
Nest, Feathers, Bird eggs, Old jewelry
Papers (Music, 3¼" x 3¼" collage)
Accu-Cut (Die cut machine, Bird die)
The Ultimate! glue

INSTRUCTIONS:

1. Die cut a bird from Grungeboard and paint it with Crackle paint. Let dry.
2. Ink the bird and music paper with Distress inks.
3. Glue music paper to the bird.
4. Remove the glass from frame and glue interesting collage paper to the backing.
5. Glue nest to frame. Glue the bird above the nest.
6. Embellish with feathers, eggs and old jewelry pieces.

Earring Holder Instructions

1. Spread gathers in the skirt evenly.

2. Glue skirt to dress form.

3. Slide keys and muse tokens on trinket pins and hang from skirt.

Earring Holder

by Donna Goss

At last, I can keep all my earrings together in the same place! No more digging to the bottom of the jewelry box. Best of all, this art has one-of-a-kind personality - like me!

SIZE: 6" x 19"

MATERIALS:

idea-ology Trinkets:
Swirls from Grungeboard Elements
6 Trinket Pins
2 long brads, 2 word keys
Assorted Foliage flowers & leaves
2 word tokens, 6 Sprocket Gears
2 small Game Spinners
Tiny Attacher stapler

Ranger:
Distress ink pads (Peeled Paint, Broken China, Spiced Marmalade)
Adirondack acrylic paints (Lettuce, Stream, Terra Cotta)
Blending tools

howdoyouglue.com
6" x 19" wood dress form

Artistic Wire 12" Gunmetal wire
Black plastic window screen (12" x 61", 12" x 16")
15" Black ½" wide ribbon
Gesso, Paint brush
Needle, Thread, Hot glue gun

INSTRUCTIONS:

1. **Dress Form:** Apply several coats of Gesso, letting dry between coats. Dry brush each color of acrylic paint in sections overlapping other colors. Let dry.
2. Paint base and pole Terra Cotta. Let dry.
3. Gather small piece of Black screen together by hand and drape it over the shoulder. Staple ends together to hold at waist.
4. **Skirt:** Thread the long edge of large screen onto wire in a gathering manner. Twist end of wire together on back of dress form at waist. Spread gathers evenly. Staple ends of screen in back to close skirt.
5. Sew or glue the ruffled ribbon around the waist to hide the wire.
6. Color grungeboard swirls with Distress inks and glue to dress form.
7. Assemble leaves and flowers from foliage set using brads. Glue in place.
8. Slide keys and muse tokens on trinket pins and hang from skirt. Layer gears with spinner and secure with brads. Hang from skirt with Trinket Pins.

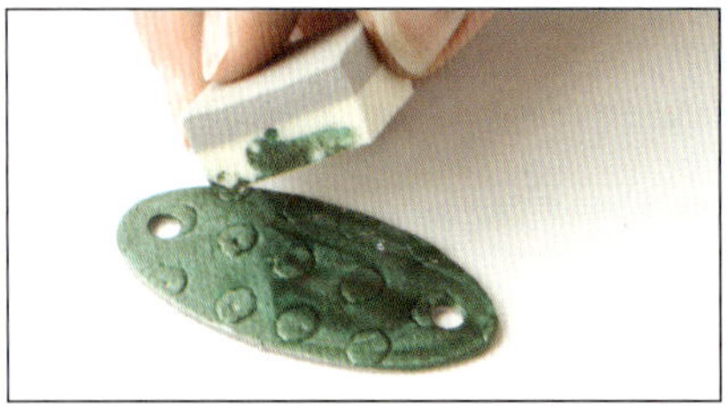

1. Sponge a Grungeboard nameplate with Broken China ink. Let dry.

2. Paint a Grungeboard flourish Gold with a Dabber. Let dry.

Swirls Wall Art

by Karen Wells

Subtly inviting, like a whisper, this artwork draws you in for a closer look. Soft colors create a gentle serenity of softness for your home.

SIZE: 5" x 7¾"

MATERIALS:

idea-ology Trinkets: Flourish & Nameplate from Grungeboard Elements Swirls, Word Tag, Mini brad, Flourish Mask, 2 Hinge Clips, 6½" Link Chain

Ranger: Distress inks (Broken China, Denim), Adirondack Gold Dabber, Claudine Hellmuth Sticky Back Canvas, Cut n' Dry sponge

Maya Road Maya Mist (Garnet, Copper Metallic)

Foamcore board, Decorative fibers, Background papers, 5" x 7¾" Red cardstock

Jewelry pliers, *The Ultimate!* glue, E6000 glue, Red liner tape

INSTRUCTIONS:

1. Place masks on canvas and mist. Let dry. Cover foamcore with canvas.
2. Sponge Grungeboard nameplate with Broken China ink. Let dry. Thread yarn through tag and wrap around canvas. Tie on side. Attach brad to word tag and glue to nameplate with E6000.
3. Layer background papers and adhere to cardstock.
4. Paint Grungeboard flourish Gold. Let dry. Sponge with Denim ink. Cut flourish in half and glue to card.
5. Attach hinge clips to top of card. Attach chain link to hole in each hinge clip.

Because Grungeboard is flexible and washable, it's perfect for embellishing clothes and totes.

Now is the time to re-cycle and create fresh, new looks with Grungeboard! After you finish, it is best to handwash your projects inside out; air dry and don't iron.

Grungeboard takes all kinds of fabric markers and paints... so unleash your inner design diva!

Stylish Crop Pants

by Judy Ross

MATERIALS:
idea-ology Trinkets: Grungeboard Plain
Denim crop pants
Blumenthal Lansing Co.
Buttons (4 'celebrate love', 1" Green)
CraftersWorkshop.com Sunflower stencil
Rubber stamps
Hero Arts Italian Poetry background,
Stampers Anonymous Tim Holtz
Fairytale Frenzy
AccuCut (diecut machine, Flower #1 die)
Tsukineko Black StazOn ink
Plaid FolkArt Fresh Foliage fabric paint
Fabric Brush Markers
Light Green, Dark Green, Neon Yellow, Blue, Hot Pink, Orange, Purple
Jacquard: Lumiere Citrine paint;
Tee Juice pens (Emerald Green, Purple, Orange)
Duncan Scribbles shiny
Lime Green 3D paint
Washable ribbon, Black thread, Needle
We R Memory Keepers
Crop-A-Dile hole punch, Paper piercer
Beacon Adhesives
Fabri-tac permanent adhesive

INSTRUCTIONS:
TIP: Use old ties for the belt and trim.
1. Place a stencil on the pants and paint with Fresh Foliage. Let dry.
2. Die-cut assorted flowers from Grungeboard.
3. Color the flowers with markers and highlight the colors with Lumiere paints. Let dry.
4. Stamp designs and let dry.
5. Punch holes around the edge of the large bottom flowers.
6. Whipstitch ribbon through the holes.
7. Glue end of ribbon behind each flower.
8. Layer flower petals and poke holes in the center. Sew flowers together and embellish the center with a button.
9. Position flowers and glue in place.
10. Sew buttons in place.

1. Paint Grungeboard flowers. Punch holes around the edges of the large flowers.

2. Whipstitch ribbon around the edges of flowers, through the holes.

Holiday Memories

by Judy Ross

Clear fragments become the focal point Christmas tree on the cover of this memory book, but fragments are so versatile you can apply this idea to any occasion. Capture the magic of a birthday party or design a frame and encase a special picture on your scrapbooking page.

Let your imagination run wild with fragments! Color them with alcohol inks to make unusual mosaics. Stamp on them with StazOn inks. Enjoy the adventure as you discover the wonderful possibilities!

SIZE: 8½" x 10"

MATERIALS:

idea-ology Trinkets: 7 sheets of Grungepaper, each 8½" x 10",
11 Clear acrylic square Fragments, Fragment tag, Ornate Plate
Me & My BIG Ideas Noel papers
Assorted ribbons
7gypsies Red book knob,
Just Rite self-inking stamp,
Zutter (Bind-It-All machine, two ½ Black coils with 3 rings each)
We R Memory Keepers Crop-A-Dile hole punch
Ranger Glossy Accents glue

INSTRUCTIONS:

1. Cover both sides of Grungepaper with scrapbooking papers.
2. Choose a front and back cover.
3. Adhere photos to fragments and fragments to cover with Glossy Accents to form a Christmas tree.
4. Finish tree with knob and trunk fragment.
5. Glue ornate plate and stamp.
6. Computer print label for fragment tag. Adhere to tag with Glossy Accents.
7. Tie tag to book cover with ribbon.
8. Design pages for book.
9. Punch holes for cover and pages.
10. Attach black coils, assemble book, and close coils.

1. Cover a Clear Fragment with Glossy Accents glue then place it on top of a photo. Let it dry.

2. Cut around the fragment and photo with scissors.

1. Apply 2 coats of Black gesso to the frame. Let dry.

2. Spread a thin coat of glass bead texture gel in random areas. Let dry.

Paint portions of the frame lightly with Off-White, letting some Black show through. Let dry.

3. Protect White areas with paper towels. Spray Color Wash. Remove towels and let dry.

4. Repeat spray process to make the color darker if desired.

5. Apply Mahogany Crackle paint. Let dry. Brush Off-White paint across the top of the embossed letter.

Wood Frame

by Darlia Hobbs

Layers of paints and texture give this frame a touchable appeal, proving you don't have to embellish heavily to make something that is interesting to the eye and attractive in your home.

SIZE: 8" x 8"

MATERIALS:

idea-ology Trinkets: 2 Sprocket Gears, Small Game Spinner, Word Token, Word Key, Mini Brad
Ranger: Adirondack Color Wash (Pesto, Terra Cotta), Aged Mahogany Distress Crackle paint
8" x 8" unfinished wood frame with a 3½" x 3½" opening
Acrylic paints (Off White, Taupe), Rubber stamps, Black archival ink pad
Golden (Glass Bead Texture Gel, Matte heavy gel, Light molding paste)
Krylon UV Resistant Clear Acrylic spray coating
Black gesso, 1" wide paint brush, Plastic palette knife, Toothpick, Paper towels

INSTRUCTIONS:

1. Apply 2 coats of Black gesso to the frame. Let dry.
2. Spread a thin coat of glass bead texture gel in random areas, especially in the corner. Let dry.
3. Apply a section of light molding paste with a palette knife. Press a stenciled letter into the wet paste. Remove the letter and allow the embossed area to dry.
4. Adhere metal embellishments with matte heavy gel. Let dry.
5. Paint portions of the frame with Off-White acrylic, letting some Black show through and brushing lightly over the glass bead areas. Let dry.
6. Tear 6" - 8" pieces of paper towel, and position as desired to protect White areas. Spray Color Wash. Remove paper towels. Let dry. The color will lighten, so you can protect the White areas with paper towels again and spray a little again to darken the color. Dab a little off with a paper towel. Let dry.
7. Apply Mahogany Crackle paint. Let dry (it will crackle when it dries).
8. Stamp Black words and images as desired.
9. Add touches of Taupe acrylic paint to areas as desired. Wipe some areas with a paper towel to reveal textures.
10. Lightly brush Off-White paint across the top of the embossed letter allowing color to show in the recessed areas.
11. Spray with 3 coats of Krylon to protect the textures.

Collage Shapes

by Donna Perrotta

Be creative and have fun decorating delightful shapes to make personalized gifts.

MATERIALS:
idea-ology Trinkets: Grungeboard shapes,
Keys, Name Plates, Gears, Corners,
Foliage, Spinners, Assorted Findings & Charms
Ranger: Rubber Stamp ink
Alcohol inks, Color Wash spray, Mixatives,
Adirondack acrylic paints, Stickles, Cut'n Dry foam
Brushes, foam paint dabbers, Paper towels
Wood or Resin shape from a home dec or wood department)
Hot glue and Goop glue, Pliers to shape metal pieces

Ideas for Decorating

1. Color a wood or resin shape with acrylic paint. Let paint dry.

2. Stain the shape by spraying a light coating of Color Wash on it.

3. Wipe off excess Color Wash with a paper towel. Let it dry.

4. Optional: Drip Alcohol inks or Mixatives over the shape. Let dry.

5. Shape metal corners into cones and cover bird beaks or wing tips.

6. Color metal trinkets with Adirondack acrylics. Glue to shape.

7. Add additional Grungeboard shapes and trinkets with glue.

Metal Plaques

MATERIALS for pages 17 - 18:
idea-ology Trinkets: Grungepaper, Grungeboard shapes, Clear Fragments, Salvage Stickers, Assorted Findings & Fasteners
Ranger: Rubber Stamp ink
Glossy Accents glue, Perfect Pearls,
Alcohol Ink Applicator, Alcohol Blending Solution
Alcohol inks: Black, Butterscotch, Rust
Distress Clear Embossing Ink, Embossing Powder,
Distress Ink, Heat Gun, Blending foam
Design Originals Distressables images on CD (Papers, Frames, Rulers, Transparency Images)
Heidi Swapp Bird Ghost shapes
House of 3.com Bird Cage Image from Digital Warehouse collection Bird Cage Brush Kit
K&Company (Life's Journey Cardstock Die-Cuts: Ephemera)
Creative Imaginations Marah Johnson Play Cards papers
3 Wood 5¼" x 7½" boards
Melissa Frances Heaven Sent Wings Applique Set
Ten Seconds Studio (#5 Paper stump, Metal Tools)
Metal Tape, Sanding block
The Ultimate! glue!

see a large photo on pages 18 - 19

Basic Instructions for Metal Plaques

1. Create a layout on a wood board with selected Grungeboard and other cardstock shapes.

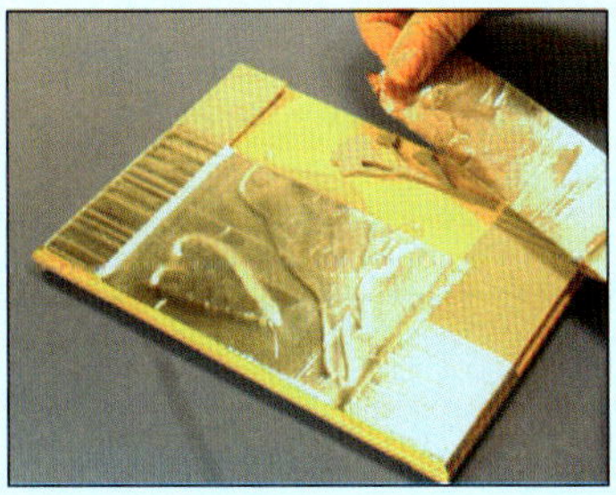

2. Cover board and selections with metal tape strips, alternating the directions as you work.

3. Use a paper stump to rub and burnish the metal tape and create outlines around the shapes.

4. Create texture by rubbing and rolling with various metal tools.

5. Add color and age by applying alcohol ink with an Ink Applicator.

Apply colors of alcohol ink to the metal surface.

6. Lightly sand away excess color build up.

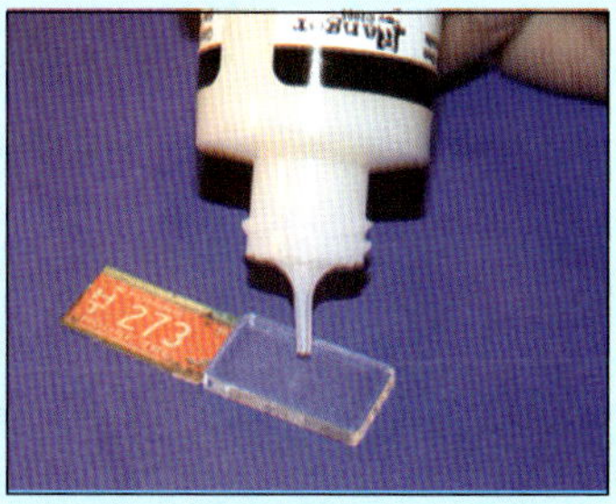

7. Apply Glossy Accents to a clear fragment and place it on a paper image. Let dry.

Cut excess paper away from the edges of the fragment with a craft knife or scissors.

8. Glue fragments and assorted findings in place. Attach fasteners.

9. Apply alcohol ink to an applicator to color the wings.

Apply more colors of alcohol ink.

Metal Collage Plaques

by Michael Jack Putman & Lesley Fisher

We love all things nostalgic, old, rusty and romantic. Combining these elements into a unified whole is an enjoyable adventure that we are grateful to share. You never know what you will find or who you will meet on your artistic journey, but you must always expect the unexpected!

We hope you enjoy these pieces and dare to explore the unlimited possibilities and untapped sources of your own talent.

SIZE: 5¼" x 7½"

continued from instructions on page 17

10. Add shine to a wing shape by brushing on Perfect Pearls.

11. **Leather-look tag:** Attach a key or word tag to a chain link with a jump ring.

Suppliers - Most craft and variety stores carry an excellent assortment of supplies. If you need something special, ask your local store to contact the following companies.

IDEA-OLOGY & GRUNGEBOARD
Advantus Corp.
www.advantus.com

Tim Holtz® is a registered trademark of Tim Holtz LLC.
Idea-ology™ is a trademark of Tim Holtz LLC.
All Tim Holtz® idea-ology™ products are manufactured and distributed by Advantus Corp.

INKS
Ranger Inks, Adirondack acrylic paints, Alcohol Inks, Color Wash, Cut'n Dry foam, Perfect Pearls, Stickles, Mixatives
www.rangerink.com